Washington

by the Capstone Press
Geography Department

CAPSTONE BOOKS

an imprint of Capstone Press
Mankato, Minnesota

Capstone Books are published by Capstone Press
151 Good Counsel Drive, P.O. Box 669, Mankato, Minnesota 56002
http://www.capstone-press.com

Library of Congress Cataloging-in-Publication Data
Washington/by the Capstone Press Geography Department
p. cm.--(One Nation)
Includes bibliographical references and index.
Summary: Gives an overview of the state of Washington, including its
history, geography, people, and living conditions.
ISBN 1-56065-441-4
1. Washington (State)--Juvenile literature. [1. Washington (State).]
I. Capstone Press. Geography Dept. II. Series.
F891.3.W37 1996
979.7--dc20

96-23438
CIP
AC

Photo Credits
G. Alan Nelson, cover, 34
Greg Vaughn, 11, 16, 18, 22, 30, 37
James Rowan, 5 (right), 6, 8, 15, 25, 26, 32
Root Resources/Ruth A. Smith, 21; Pat Wadecki, 28
Unicorn/Nancy Ferguson, 4 (left); Richard Dippold, 4 (right);
    Dede Gilman, 5 (left)

2 3 4 5 6 04 03 02 01 00

Table of Contents

Words in **boldface** type in the text are defined
in the Glossary in the back of this book.

Fast Facts about Washington

State Flag

Location: In the Pacific Northwest region of the United States
Size: 71,302 square miles (185,385 square kilometers)

Population: 5,756,361 (1999 U.S. Census Bureau estimate)
Capital: Olympia
Date admitted to the Union: November 11, 1889; the 42nd state

Willow goldfinch

Coast rhododendron

Largest cities:
Seattle,
Spokane,
Tacoma,
Bellevue,
Everett,
Federal Way,
Vancouver,
Lakewood,
Yakima,
Bellingham

Nickname: The Evergreen State
State bird: Willow goldfinch
State flower:
Coast
rhododendron
State tree:
Western
hemlock
State song:
"Washington,
My Home," by
Helen Davis

Western hemlock

5

Chapter 1

Washington's Volcanoes

In March 1980, smoke began to rise from Mount St. Helens. Small earthquakes made the ground rumble. Many people drove to the mountain to get a better look. **Geologists** warned residents and visitors to leave the area.

On May 18, at 8:32 A.M. Pacific time, Mount St. Helens **erupted**. A huge cloud of hot **ash** rose 10 miles (16 kilometers) into the sky. The ash blew across the Cascade Mountains.

Mount St. Helens erupted in 1980, leaving the land around it in a mess.

Mount Rainier is an active volcano, but it has not erupted for more than 2,000 years.

Hot gas from the blast blew down forests. A landslide of mud rushed into Spirit Lake and the Toutle River. Thousands of animals were killed. Sixty-two people were dead or missing.

The eruption destroyed about 1,300 feet (390 meters) of the mountaintop. Mount St. Helens was once Washington's fifth tallest mountain. Now it is in 13th place.

Volcanoes in the Cascades

Mount St. Helens is one of the Cascade's volcanic peaks. Mount Rainier is north of Mount St. Helens. This still-active volcano last erupted 2,200 years ago. Mount Baker is an active volcano in the northern Cascades. Steam sometimes rises from its crater.

Volcanic ash makes good fertilizer. Trees, flowers, and grasses are growing again near Mount St. Helens. Many animals have moved back into the area.

Tourists have returned, too. The Mount St. Helens National Volcanic Monument was established in 1982. Visitors there can see what happens when a volcano erupts.

Other Attractions

Washington has great natural beauty. Three national parks and parts of nine national forests cover the state. Water sports are popular.

Washington's cities and towns are among the nation's best places to live. Seattle is the home of the grunge sound made famous by Soundgarden, Nirvana, and Pearl Jam.

Chapter 2

The Land

Washington lies in the Pacific Northwest region of the United States. The Pacific Ocean forms the state's western border. Washington's lowest point is at sea level along the coast.

Mountain Ranges

Large mountain ranges cut through Washington. Most of the mountains are snow-capped. **Glaciers** cover their slopes.

The Olympic Mountains stand in northwestern Washington. The western side of the mountains gets more than 140 inches (357 centimeters) of rain each year. Olympic National Park has a big

Mountains and glaciers are some of Washington's most beautiful land forms.

rain forest. The country's largest western hemlocks, red cedars, and noble firs grow there.

The Cascade Mountains are in west-central Washington. They stretch from Canada south into Oregon. Mount Rainier is in the Cascades. This volcanic peak is Washington's highest point. It stands 14,410 feet (4,392 meters) above sea level.

Douglas fir trees grow in the western Cascades. Coal, gold, and copper lie in the eastern Cascades.

The Rocky Mountains cross northeastern Washington. Gold, silver, lead, zinc, and magnesium are found there.

Puget Sound Lowland

The Puget Sound lowland lies between the Olympic and Cascade mountains. Puget Sound is connected to the Pacific Ocean by the Strait of Juan de Fuca.

Puget Sound has many good harbors. Large cities grew around the harbors. Seattle is the largest city. It lies on Puget Sound. So does Olympia, the state capital. These and other cities on Puget Sound are important shipping centers.

Columbia Plateau

The Columbia Plateau stretches across eastern Washington. Dry plains and rugged hills mark the land. The Columbia River winds through the plateau before turning east and emptying into the Pacific Ocean.

Irrigation makes the plateau's western river valleys good for farming. Fruits and vegetables grow in the Yakima, Walla Walla, and Wenatchee valleys.

The Snake River runs through the southeastern part of the plateau. Grain crops grow well there. Beef cattle graze on its grasses.

Climate

The high Cascade Mountains stop the winds that blow east from the Pacific. Clouds moving eastward drop their rain before reaching the Cascades.

West of the Cascades, the climate is humid and rainy. Summers are cool, and winters are warm. East of the Cascades, the climate is drier. Eastern Washington also has warmer summers and colder winters.

Wildlife

Mountain lions and mountain goats live in the Olympic Mountains. Antelope and deer graze on the Columbia Plateau. Lynx live in the northern forests.

Seattle, Washington's largest city, is on Puget Sound.

Sea lions and seals are common on the Pacific coast. Whales **migrate** in northern coastal waters.

Terns, eagles, and cormorants fly overhead. Chinook and sockeye salmon swim in Washington's rivers.

Chapter 3

The People

Washington is one of the fastest growing states in the nation. Between 1980 and 1990, the state grew by more than 700,000 people. By 1994, almost 500,000 more people lived in Washington.

Some of Washington's newest residents come from other states. Others come from foreign countries. Many newcomers have moved from California. They want to live in a less-crowded state. In 1994, more than 18,000 **immigrants** moved to Washington. The largest numbers came from Canada, Germany, Mexico, and Sweden.

Washington is one of the fastest growing states.

About half of Washington's population lives around Puget Sound.

More than 75 percent of the people live in cities. About half of Washington's population lives around Puget Sound. Spokane and Yakima are large cities in eastern Washington.

Washington's Largest Population Group

About 89 percent of Washington's people are white. Many of them are **descendants** of Washington's first white settlers. These early settlers started arriving from midwestern states in the 1850s. Most of them were farmers and loggers. They had come to America from Germany, Norway, Sweden, Ireland, and England.

Asian Americans

Asians began moving into Washington later in the 1800s. Most were Japanese or Chinese. Many worked in the mines and on farms. Later, many of them settled in Washington's cities.

Japanese Americans suffered during World War II (1939-1945). The United States was at war with Japan. The government moved 13,000 of Washington's Japanese Americans. They were moved to camps in other states. The government feared that Japanese Americans might act as spies for Japan. There was no evidence that they were ever disloyal to the United States.

More than 4 percent of Washington's population is now Asian American. Recent immigrants have come from Korea, Vietnam, and the Philippines.

Many Asian Americans live in **ethnic** neighborhoods. The largest of these is Seattle's

International District. Restaurants, shops, and museums there give glimpses of Asian culture.

African Americans

Washington is home to about 150,000 African Americans. The first African American to settle in Washington was George Bush. He and his family arrived in 1845.

Most African Americans moved to Washington after World War II. Jobs in the state's growing manufacturing plants attracted them.

Hispanic Americans

Washington's Hispanics come from Mexico and other Spanish-speaking countries. Many of them are seasonal workers. They work in the state's fruit orchards and vegetable fields.

Some Hispanic families have settled permanently in Washington. Hispanics now make up about 4 percent of the state's population.

Native Americans

Washington's Native American population is the sixth highest in the country. About 81,000

Many people live in Washington because of the weather.

Native Americans live in the state. The Yakima, Lummi, and Quinault are the largest tribes.

Most make their home on one of 27 **reservations** in Washington. The Colville and Yakima reservations are the largest ones.

Chapter 4

Washington History

People have lived in Washington for at least 12,000 years. **Ancestors** of today's Native Americans had moved into Washington by the 1500s.

The Chinook, Nisqually, and Quinault built villages west of the Cascades. They hunted deer and caught salmon.

Explorers

In 1792, both the United States and Great Britain claimed Washington belonged to them. George Vancouver explored Puget Sound for England. Robert Gray, an American, entered the Columbia River from the Pacific Ocean.

Native Americans were the first to live in Washington.

In 1805, Meriwether Lewis and William Clark crossed the Rocky Mountains. Lewis and Clark followed the Columbia River to its **mouth** on the Pacific. The trip helped America's claim to the Pacific Northwest.

American and English fur trading companies moved into Washington in the early 1800s. They traded with Native Americans for beaver pelts. The companies set up trading posts and forts. John Jacob Astor was an American trader. He founded Fort Okanogan in 1811. This was the first American settlement in Washington.

Washington Becomes American

In 1818, the United States and England agreed that both American and British settlers could move into the area. At that time, Washington was part of the Oregon Country.

John McLoughlin headed the British Hudson's Bay Company. He built Fort Vancouver in 1825. It was the first European settlement in Washington.

Many Americans wanted the United States to own all of Oregon Country. In 1846, Britain and

Fort Vancouver was the first European settlement in Washington. It was built by John McLoughlin.

the United States drew a boundary. The 49th **parallel** became the border between Washington and Canada. By 1850, more than 1,000 people lived in Washington.

In 1853, the United States Congress created the Washington Territory. Olympia became the capital.

Toward Statehood

Thousands of farmers, loggers, and miners moved into Washington. They built towns along the rivers. The new settlers pushed the Native Americans onto reservations.

Railroads from the Midwest and the East reached Washington in the 1880s and1890s. New settlers came to the state on trains. In 1889, Washington became the 42nd state. The 1890 census counted 357,232 Washingtonians.

Growth in the New State

Irrigation projects started on the Columbia Plateau. Farmers moved to the newly fertile land. Fruit orchards and vegetable fields bloomed.

After the railroad reached Seattle, it became a great port city. During the Alaska Gold Rush in 1897 and 1898, the city **outfitted** miners for their journey north.

Railroads made traveling easier and faster than wagons.

Thousands of workers built the Grand Coulee Dam.

World Wars and the Great Depression

During World War I (1914-1918), the country needed Washington's lumber, food, and ships. Camp Lewis was built as a military training base.

When the war ended, factories slowed production. In February 1919, about 60,000 Seattle workers walked off their jobs. They wanted better pay.

The Great Depression (1929-1939) hit Washingtonians hard. Many workers lost their jobs. The United States government started projects to help the unemployed. Thousands of workers built the Grand Coulee and Bonneville dams.

World War II (1939-1945) helped end the Depression. Ships built in Washington helped win the war. A bomber built by Seattle's Boeing Company dropped an atomic bomb on Hiroshima, Japan. That brought an end to the war.

Recent Growth and Problems

Since the 1940s, more and more people have moved to Washington. Many took jobs in the logging industry. Puget Sound's suburbs became good-sized cities. Electronics and computer-**software** companies started in these new cities.

This growth and change caused many problems. Pollution increased along Puget Sound and the Columbia River. Logging known as **clear cutting** destroyed much of Washington's forests. In the future, Washington plans to take better care of the environment.

Chapter 5

Washington Business

More Washington people have jobs in service businesses than any other industry. Manufacturing, agriculture, and fishing are other important state industries.

Service Industries

Trade and tourism are major Washington service industries. Much of Washington's trade is with Asian nations. The state's forest products are important trade goods.

Seattle-based companies such as Nordstrom and Starbucks also help Washington's trade. They have stores throughout the nation.

Washington manufactures many wood and paper products.

Shipyards play an important role in Washington industry.

Tourists spend about $5 billion in Washington each year. Restaurants, hotels, and museums are part of the tourist industry.

Manufacturing

Transportation items are Washington's most important products. The Boeing Company leads the nation in manufacturing passenger airplanes.

Shipyards in Bremerton, Seattle, and Tacoma build freighters, barges, tugs, and passenger ferries.

Computer **hardware** and software are also made in Washington. Microsoft Corporation in Redmond is the world's leading software company.

Washington field and forest products are also prepared for sale. Factories pack, can, and freeze fruits, vegetables, and fish. Lumber mills produce wood for making furniture and for home construction. Pulp mills make paper and cardboard.

Agriculture

Timber is Washington's main agricultural product. Western hemlock and Douglas firs lead the list for cut trees.

Wheat, barley, asparagus, carrots, beans, and peas are leading crops. Washington is the top apple-growing state. It is a world leader at growing daffodil and iris **bulbs**. Dairy farms operate in southwestern Washington and near Puget Sound.

Fishing

Chinook, coho, sockeye, and pink salmon lead Washington's fish catch. Halibut, oysters, crabs, and tuna are also caught in Washington's waters.

Chapter 6

Seeing the Sights

W ashington has snow-capped mountains and evergreen forests. Waves pound the cliffs along the rugged Pacific seacoast. Washington's small towns and cities have many other attractions.

Western Washington

Port Angeles is northwestern Washington's largest town. It is the headquarters for Olympic National Park. Hikers can follow more than 600 miles (960 kilometers) of trails in the park.

Mount Olympus in the Olympic Mountains is the park's highest peak. The Blue Glacier covers its slopes.

To the south is Grays Harbor. The twin logging towns of Aberdeen and Hoquiam sit on the harbor's northeastern tip. A **replica** of one of Robert Gray's ships sits in Aberdeen's harbor. Hoquiam's Castle

The forests of Olympic National Park have trails for hikers.

stands in Hoquiam. A rich lumberman built the 20-room mansion in 1897.

Long Island is farther south in Willapa Bay. The island is a **refuge** for bear, deer, and elk. A 4,000-year-old grove of cedar trees is also protected there.

Vancouver lies southeast along the Columbia River. This is the oldest town in Washington. Fort Vancouver has been rebuilt. Visitors there can view life in the fur trade at a Hudson's Bay Company post.

Washington's Northern Islands

Ferries from Washington's mainland carry passengers to its islands. The San Juan Islands lie north of Puget Sound. The largest fishing port in the islands is called Friday Harbor. Whale-watchers often spot **orcas** from Lime Kiln State Park.

Whidbey Island lies to the south in Puget Sound. It is the nation's longest island outside of Hawaii. Visitors enjoy the peace and quiet of Whidbey's villages.

Cities on Puget Sound

Seattle lies on the eastern shore of Puget Sound. Many of the city's earliest buildings lie 30 feet (nine meters) under its streets. Visitors take the Underground

The Seattle skyline shows the very tall Space Needle.

Tour to see old Seattle. Others take an elevator to the top of the Space Needle. It is 607 feet (182 meters) high. This tower was built for the 1962 World's Fair.

One of Seattle's most popular sites is Pike Place Market. Early in the morning, shoppers line the market's sidewalks and alleys. They buy fresh fruit, fish, and vegetables.

Tacoma lies south of Seattle. One of the world's longest suspension bridges crosses Puget Sound there. The Tacoma Narrows Bridge is 5,450 feet (1,635 meters) long.

Olympia is at Puget Sound's southern end. This city is the state capital. Visitors come in the spring to see the cherry trees on the capitol grounds.

Central Washington

The Cascade Mountains cut through the center of Washington. Skiers and hikers can explore about 320 glaciers in North Cascades National Park.

Lake Chelan is south of the park. It is a narrow, winding lake in the Wenatchee National Forest. Hang gliders take off from the lake's steep bluffs.

Yakima is farther south. It is central Washington's largest city. Each March, the city hosts a celebration called Chocolate Fantasy. Chocolate makers from around the country give out samples of chocolate.

Eastern Washington

Grand Coulee Dam is on the Columbia River. It is the world's largest concrete dam. The dam is about a mile (1.6 kilometers) long and 50 stories high. On summer nights, a laser show lights it up.

Franklin D. Roosevelt Lake lies behind the dam. This is Washington's largest lake. Fishers, swimmers, and water-skiers enjoy its waters.

Spokane is southeast of the dam. It is close to the Idaho border. The city takes great pride in Riverfront Park. Concerts in summer and ice skating in winter attract large crowds. Young people like the roller coaster and Ferris wheel.

Washington Time Line

10,000 B.C.—The first people arrive in Washington.

1792—Robert Gray, an American, reaches the mouth of the Columbia River; George Vancouver explores Puget Sound for Great Britain.

1805—Lewis and Clark canoe down the Columbia River to the Pacific Ocean.

1811—Fort Okanogan, the first United States settlement in Washington, is built.

1818—The United States and Great Britain agree to share the settlement of the Oregon Country.

1825—British traders build Fort Vancouver on the Columbia River.

1846—The United States and Great Britain agree on the 49th parallel as the border between Washington and Canada.

1853—The United States Congress creates the Washington Territory.

1863—The Washington Territory includes the modern boundaries of the state of Washington.

1887—The first railroad from the eastern United States reaches Washington.

1889—Washington becomes the 42nd state.

1910—Washington grants women the right to vote.

1926—In Seattle, Bertha Landes becomes the first woman elected mayor of a major United States city.

1942—Grand Coulee Dam begins operation.

1962—Seattle hosts the World's Fair.

1974—Spokane hosts the Expo '74 World's Fair.

1977—Dixy Lee Ray becomes Washington's first woman governor.

1980—Mount St. Helens erupts.

1989—Norman Rice is elected Seattle's first African-American mayor.

1994—Harold Moss becomes Tacoma's first African-American mayor.

Famous Washingtonians

William Boeing (1881-1956) Engineer who founded Seattle-based Boeing Airplane Company in 1916.

Carol Channing (1923-) Actress and singer who starred in *Hello Dolly*; born in Seattle.

Bing Crosby (1903-1977) World-famous singer and Academy Award-winning movie star; born in Tacoma and grew up in Spokane.

Bonnie Dunbar (1949-) Astronaut who took part in the 1985 Challenger space mission; born in Sunnyside.

Bill Gates (1955-) Computer programmer who founded Microsoft Corporation; born in Seattle.

Jimi Hendrix (1942-1970) Rock guitarist and singer who formed the Jimi Hendrix Experience; wrote "Purple Haze" and "Fire"; born in Seattle.

Frank Herbert (1920-1986) Writer of the *Dune* science-fiction books; born in Tacoma.

Chief Joseph (1840-1904) Leader of the Nez Perce Indians; spent his last years on the Colville Indian Reservation.

Gary Larson (1950-) Cartoonist who created "The Far Side"; born in Tacoma.

Patty Murray (1950-) Teacher who was elected as a United States senator from Washington in 1992; born in Seattle.

Craig T. Nelson (1946-) Actor who starred as the coach in television's *Coach*; born in Spokane.

Dixy Lee Ray (1914-1994) Marine zoologist who became Washington's first woman governor (1977-1981); born in Tacoma.

Ryne Sandburg (1959-) All-Star second-baseman for the Chicago Cubs; born in Spokane.

Seathl (1786-1866) Chief of several Native American tribes around Puget Sound who befriended early white settlers; born near present-day Seattle.

Adam West (1928-) Actor who played Batman in the 1960s television series; born in Walla Walla.

Narcissa Whitman (1808-1847) Pioneer and missionary who established, with her husband Marcus Whitman (1802-1847), a mission for Native Americans in Walla Walla; was killed in a raid by Cayuse Indians.

Glossary

ancestor—a person from whom one is descended, such as a grandmother or a great-grandfather

ash—hot smoke and dust blown from an erupting volcano

bulb—the rounded root of certain plants

clear cutting—completely stripping hillsides of trees

descendant—a person born to a family

erupt—to burst suddenly

ethnic—relating to a group of people with the same cultural background

glacier—a huge, slow-moving sheet of ice

geologist—a scientist who studies the history of and changes in the earth

hardware—computer equipment such as a disk drive, monitor, or printer

immigrant—a person who comes to another country to settle

irrigation—a system of bringing water to fields and crops

migrate—to move from one region to another, usually on a seasonal basis

mouth—the place where a river empties into a larger body of water

orca—a killer whale

outfit—to furnish miners, explorers, or travelers with food, clothing, tools, and equipment

parallel—an imaginary line that measures distance from the equator

refuge—a safe place

replica—a copy

reservation—land set aside for Native Americans

software—programs run by computers

To Learn More

Hirischi, Ron. *People of Salmon and Cedar.* New York: Cobblehill Books, 1996.

Lambert, Dale and Laura Lambert. *Washington: Past and Present.* East Wenatchee, Wash.: DMI, 1998.

Nelson, Sharlene P. *Mount St. Helens National Volcanic Monument.* A True Book. Chicago: Children's Press, 1997.

Stefoff, Rebecca. *Washington.* Celebrate the States. New York: Benchmark Books, 1999.

Internet Sites

Access Washington
http://www.wa.gov
Excite Travel—Washington
http://www.excite.com/travel/countries/
    united_states/washington
Travel.org—Washington
http://travel.org/washing.html
Washington State Tourism
http://www.tourism.wa.gov

Useful Addresses

Bing Crosby Library
East 502 Boone Street
Spokane, WA 99210

Coulee Dam National Recreation Area
P.O. Box 36
Coulee Dam, WA 99116

Mount Rainier National Park Headquarters
Tahoma Woods, Star Route
Ashford, WA 98304

Underground Tour
610 First Avenue
Seattle, WA 98104

Whale Museum
62 First Street.
Friday Harbor, WA 98250

Whitman Mission National Historic Site
Route 2, Box 247
Walla Walla, WA 99362

Index